How a Caterpillar Grows Into a Butterfly

Written by
Tanya Kant

Illustrated by
Carolyn Franklin

Hold the page
up to the light
to see what's on
the other side.

children's press®

An Imprint of Scholastic Inc.

NEW YORK • TORONTO • LONDON • AUCKLAND • SYDNEY
MEXICO CITY • NEW DELHI • HONG KONG
DANBURY, CONNECTICUT

© The Salariya Book Company Ltd MMVIII
No part of this publication may be reproduced in whole or in part, or stored in a retrieval system, or transmitted in any form or by any means, electronic, mechanical, photocopying, recording, or otherwise, without written permission of the copyright holder. For information regarding permission, write to salariya@salariya.com

Published in Great Britain in 2008 by
The Salariya Book Company Ltd
25 Marlborough Place, Brighton BN1 1UB
England
www.salariya.com

ISBN-13: 978-0-531-24046-5 (lib. bdg.)   978-0-531-23800-4 (pbk.)
ISBN-10: 0-531-24046-0 (lib. bdg.)   0-531-23800-8 (pbk.)

All rights reserved.
Published in 2009 in the United States
by Children's Press
An imprint of Scholastic Inc.

A CIP catalog record for this book is available
from the Library of Congress.

Printed and bound in China.

Author: **Tanya Kant** is a graduate of the University of Sussex at Brighton, England. She specializes in writing and editing children's nonfiction, and is especially interested in natural science and history. She lives in Hove, England.

Artist: **Carolyn Franklin** graduated from Brighton College of Art with a focus on design and illustration. Since then she has worked in animation, advertising, and children's fiction and nonfiction. She has a special interest in natural history and has written many books on the subject, including *Life in the Wetlands* in the **WHAT ON EARTH?** series and *Egg to Owl* in the **CYCLES OF LIFE** series.

Consultant: **Monica Hughes** is an experienced educational advisor and author of more than one hundred books for young children. She has been head teacher of a primary school, primary advisory teacher, and senior lecturer in early childhood education.

red admiral butterfly

PAPER FROM
SUSTAINABLE
FORESTS

Contents

What Is a Butterfly?

A butterfly is an **insect**. It begins life as an egg. A caterpillar hatches from the egg. When the caterpillar is fully grown, it forms a case called a **pupa**. Inside the pupa, the caterpillar slowly changes. When it comes out, it is a beautiful butterfly.

This book is about the life of a red admiral butterfly.

All insects have six legs. An insect's body is made of three parts: a head, a **thorax**, and an **abdomen**.

antennae

A butterfly has two pairs of wings and one pair of **antennae**. Many butterflies have bright patterns on their wings.

butterfly bush

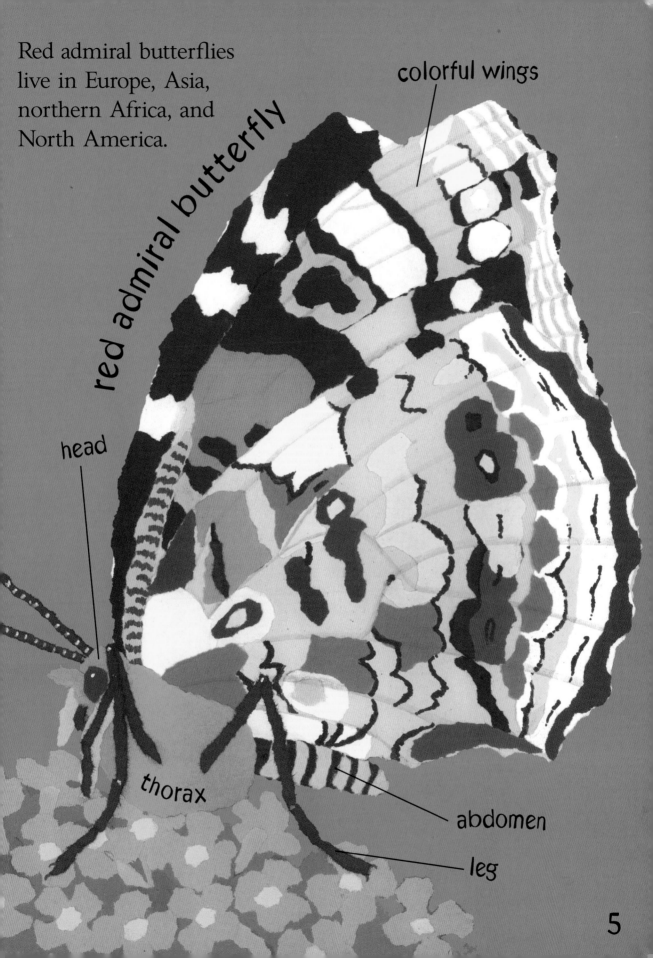

Red admiral butterflies live in Europe, Asia, northern Africa, and North America.

colorful wings

red admiral butterfly

head

thorax

abdomen

leg

5

Do Butterflies Lay Eggs?

A female butterfly lays eggs that have been **fertilized** by a male butterfly. The female butterfly lays her eggs on leaves. A tiny baby insect grows inside each egg. Red admiral eggs **hatch** after about a week. But the insect that comes out doesn't look like a butterfly! It is a caterpillar.

The caterpillar breaks through the egg.

The eggs are very sticky. They stick very firmly to the leaf so that they will not fall off.

The caterpillar pushes out of the egg.

The red admiral caterpillar is light in color at first. As it grows, it will become much darker. You can see this on the next page.

7

What Is a Caterpillar?

Even though a caterpillar will one day be a butterfly, it looks very different from a butterfly. Caterpillars have no wings. They crawl along plants using little legs.

Caterpillars can crawl upside down. They have rings of tiny hooks that they use to cling onto the underside of a leaf.

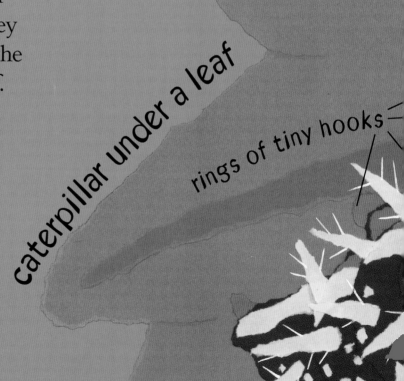

caterpillar under a leaf

rings of tiny hooks

head

legs

thorax

abdomen

9

What Do Caterpillars Eat?

Caterpillars eat green leaves so that they can grow bigger. Caterpillars can make very thin threads of **silk**. The red admiral caterpillar folds up a leaf and uses the sticky silk to stick the leaf together like a tent. Then the caterpillar hides inside the leaf and eats it bit by bit.

Caterpillars can also use their silk thread to hang from plants.

The caterpillar hides in a folded leaf.

Munch
munch

sticky silk

eaten leaf

Why Do Some Caterpillars Hide in Leaves?

Caterpillars make a juicy treat for animals such as spiders, wasps, and birds. Animals that eat other animals are called **predators**. By hiding inside a leaf, the caterpillar can protect itself from being eaten.

spider

Cheep titmouse cheep

Buzz buzz zzzzz wasp

Some caterpillars have sharp spines that protect them against predators. Others can escape from danger by dropping from a tree, using their silk like a parachute.

13

Why Does a Caterpillar Shed Its Skin?

As the caterpillar grows, its skin becomes very tight. From time to time it has to shed its skin. This is called **molting**. First, the caterpillar grows new skin under its old skin. Then the old skin splits and the caterpillar crawls out of it.

old skin splitting

leaf

caterpillar in its new skin

silk threads

How Does a Caterpillar Change Into a Butterfly?

When the caterpillar is fully grown, it gets ready to turn into a butterfly. It uses its silk to hang from a plant stem. Then it sheds its skin for the last time.

silk thread

leaf stem

old skin

After a few hours, a
hard, tough shell forms
around the caterpillar,
covering it from head
to tail. This shell is
called a pupa or **chrysalis**.
Inside the pupa, the caterpillar
slowly begins to change into
a butterfly.

pupa

Hold the page up
to the light to see
the butterfly.

17

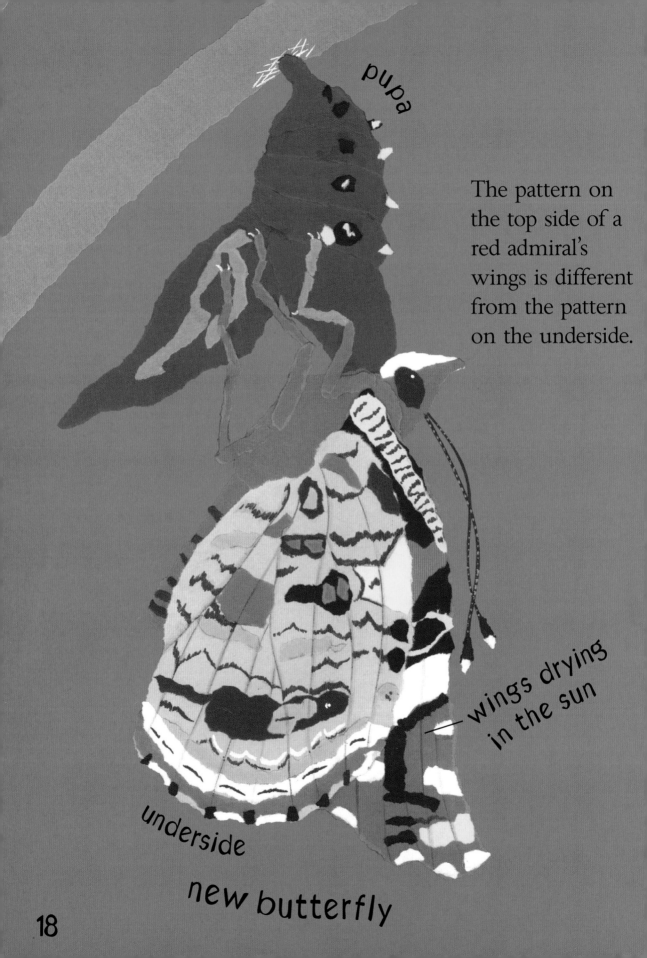

pupa

The pattern on the top side of a red admiral's wings is different from the pattern on the underside.

wings drying in the sun

underside

new butterfly

18

How Long Does it Take for a Butterfly to Form?

The pupa splits open after about three weeks. The butterfly crawls out and shakes its new wings. The butterfly waits for its wings to dry. Then it is ready to fly away.

ready to fly!

top side

Why Do Butterflies Have Patterns on Their Wings?

There are many different types, or species, of butterflies. Some butterflies have brightly colored and beautifully decorated wings. Others are more plain. Colored wings help a butterfly find a **mate** and scare off predators.

swallowtail butterfly

A butterfly's wing patterns are **symmetrical**. This means that one side is a mirror image of the other.

What Do Butterflies Eat?

Most butterflies drink the nectar of flowers. A butterfly has a long, curly tongue that it can uncoil to suck up the nectar it finds in the center of the flower.

The butterfly uncoils its tongue to suck up nectar.

Slurp slurp tongue

How Far Can a Butterfly Fly?

Some butterflies fly hundreds or thousands of miles, across countries and oceans, to find the right food or the best place to lay their eggs. This is called **migration**. Red admirals in northern Europe migrate to the Mediterranean.

One type of butterfly, called the painted lady, can fly more than 600 miles without stopping to rest.

painted lady butterfly migrating

Where Do Butterflies Go in the Winter?

Butterflies do not like cold weather. In winter, most kinds of butterflies look for a warm, dry place to sleep. Sleeping through the winter is called **hibernation**. Some butterflies hibernate in groups of tens of thousands.

snail

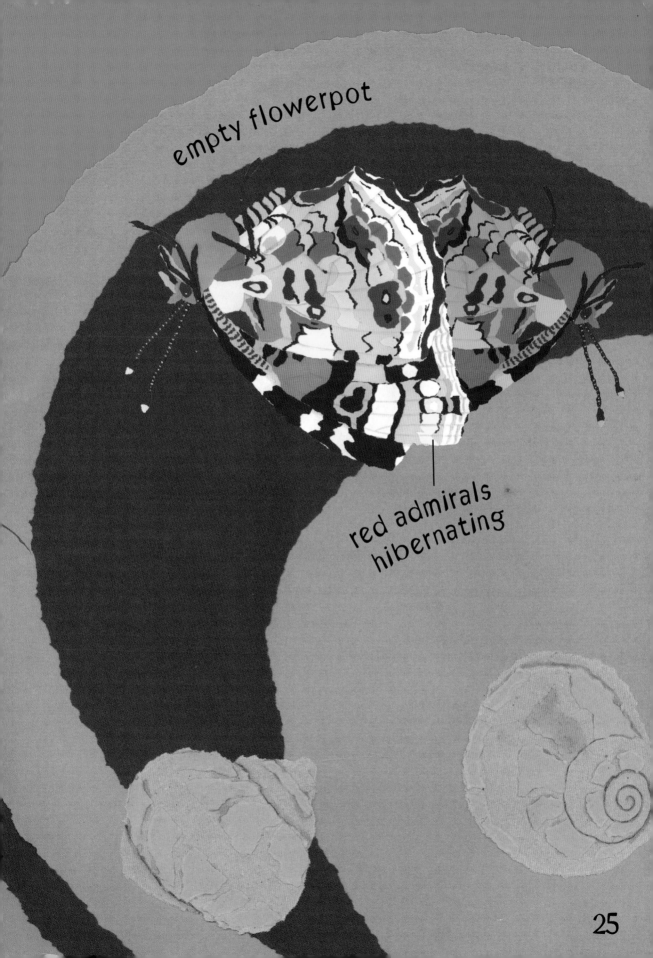

empty flowerpot

red admirals
hibernating

Butterfly Facts

What's the difference between a butterfly and a moth? A butterfly is an insect that flies during the day. It has antennae with club-shaped tips. A moth is an insect that flies mainly at night. It has antennae that are thread-like or feathery.

The largest butterfly is Queen Alexandra's birdwing butterfly of Papua New Guinea. It is 11 inches wide.

One of the smallest butterflies is the western pygmy blue from Africa. It is less than half an inch wide.

The fastest flyer is the monarch butterfly of North America. It can fly 20 miles per hour.

Butterflies beat their wings between 5 and 15 times a second.

Some butterflies live for only a few days, but others can live for several months.

The sixty-nine butterfly of South America looks as though it has the number 69 on its wings.

red admiral

owl butterfly

The owl butterfly of South America has markings on its wings that make it look like an owl. This helps to frighten away predators.

The caterpillar of the Jamaican swallowtail looks just like a bird dropping. Predators do not recognize it as a tasty meal.

Zebra butterflies from the Americas are brightly colored. They do not bother to hide, since they are poisonous and are left alone by their enemies.

The African leaf butterfly lies down among dead leaves to rest. It looks exactly like dead leaves, so predators do not see it.

brimstone butterfly

butterfly bush

Butterflies like brightly colored flowers to feed from.

Things to Do: Make Your Garden a Butterfly Garden

If you have a garden, there are many things you can do to encourage butterflies to come into it.

Butterflies like to bask in the sun on hot days. Include a big flat rock for them to rest on.

Make a hibernating box to give the butterflies a place to sleep.

Butterflies like to drink from shallow water. You could provide a bird bath, or just a container with some water in it.

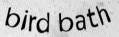
bird bath

red admiral

painted lady

Patches of tall grass or plants help the butterflies to shelter from the rain.

Life Cycle of a Butterfly

egg

newly hatched
caterpillar

adult
butterfly

pupa

full-grown
caterpillar

Words to Remember

Abdomen The tail section of an insect's body.

Antennae The feelers on an insect's head.

Chrysalis The case inside which a caterpillar turns into a butterfly.

Fertilized An egg is fertilized when a male and a female animal mate. Only a fertilized egg can become a new animal.

Hatch An egg hatches when a caterpillar comes out of it.

Hibernation Sleeping through the winter.

Insect A creature with six legs and a head, thorax, and abdomen.

Mate (noun) A partner.

Mate (verb) To join together to fertilize an egg.

Migration Moving to a different place for part of the year.

Molting Shedding an old skin and growing a new one.

Nectar A sweet substance in flowers that butterflies drink.

Predator An animal that kills and eats other animals.

Pupa Another word for chrysalis.

Silk A sticky substance produced by some insects that dries to make a very thin, strong thread.

Symmetrical The same on both sides, like a mirror image.

Thorax The middle section of an insect's body. An insect's legs are attached to its thorax.

Index